caging butterflies

ELISE FISHER

"Life: a constellation of vital phenomena—
organization, irritability, movement,
growth, reproduction, adaptation."
—Anthony Marra

"At the time, I often thought that
if I had had to live in the
trunk of a dead tree, with nothing
to do but look up at the sky
flowering overhead, little by little
I would have gotten used to it."
—Albert Camus

CHAPTERS

I. *caterpillar*

      the larva of a butterfly or moth.

II. *chrysalis*

      the pupa of a butterfly or moth; a
      transitional state.

III. *wings*

      extensions of an insect's body that
      allow it to fly.

caging butterflies

ELISE FISHER

CATERPILLAR

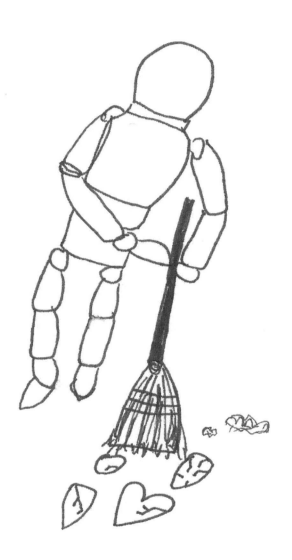

kiln

Since I was first placed in the kiln
I have adapted—
I fell in and melted a little, stuck to the wall,
but now I have let the dry heat harden me
and I eat the air that glazes me over and
finally finishes me;

I am glossy
I am new
So that you can paint me blue
and paint me black
while we both pretend I'm not matte
Press your thumb into my side,
mold me, mold me,
make me real this time.

I think to myself,
At least I didn't crack, at least I didn't break,
but even my wholeness feels like a heartache and I can't escape
the kiln inside my head, inside my room;
Each day I sweep up little clay bits of me with a broom,
surrounded by dust of what was and what could have been

I am only what I have let myself be and let you make me
It all falls from me like ash and
today I don't mind the fire
even though it burns my hand.

call me when you find me

What do you call it when
you don't know what you're feeling,
when your emotions ebb and flow,
when the only constancy you can count on is inconsistency—
Acceptance coming down from the sky like rain
until doubt knocks me over like a wave;
Happiness giving way to anxiety,
emptiness eating away at my satiety,
I don't know who to believe
out of the conflicting voices inside of me,
don't know when there will be relief
from the hole that's full of me.
Why is it that I can't seem to stay
in one place?
Back and forth,
up is down and down is up;
Spinning around so dizzily,
Call me when you find me.

waves of honey, shore of salt

my thoughts are like small boats
trying to tread oceans of honey;
all smells sweet but the voyage is so bitter

landing on a shore of salt
that makes my wounds sting
as my words tumble across the landing strip of my tongue

power is lost as trees fall,
plants shrivel upon my attempts at love,
and the sun still beats on my crooked back
while I seek shelter from my own mind

I cannot escape; I am shipwrecked.
the waves do not subside,
the light does not discriminate,
my thoughts try to bury me alive,
but everything still smells like honey

sharp things

only when I get too close
do I see that the flowers on your lips
grow among the thorns of cactuses

I am too late
every inch of my skin is pricked
but my blood is red
just like the roses you gave me—
they had thorns, too

the pit

when I see you I still feel your hands
on my body, in places I didn't want them
I remember that look,
the emptiness burning holes inside of me

I see you but I cannot look at you
because you were the first person to make me feel like
an object,
created for your convenience

when I see you, I am not myself;
I am the sum of my parts,
the pit of my stomach,
the apple of your rotten eyes

skull storm

I feel the clouds forming in my head
my mind is overcast with dark thoughts
I cannot see
and it starts to pour clear water from my bright eyes
as white lightning flashes within them

furious winds rage in my head
and swirl around my brain,
destroying everything—
until they come to you.

memories flood my mind and rise up like waves inside of me;
you beat against my fragile skull
and toss around my timid thoughts like sailboats in a hurricane.
missing you is a terrible storm,
and its lightning always strikes in the same places.

her

I see the way you look at her,
like time stops for a second when she laughs
or when she says your name
I wonder why it's still her and not me
and then I realize
I may be a great listener,
quick to learn and good with words
but I'll never have the gift
of a beauty like hers

tyranny of the majority

I see you, a flower
across the room
and I stare
level-headed, empty-handed
until my eyes become glossy
with glass tears
that fall to my feet and shatter
as I beg to look like you

false god

when I asked him what his favorite color was,
he said blue,
and I knew it, too;
he was blue
all the way through—
I thought that meant good for you,
when it really meant
he won't fight for you;
he was blue
blue
too good to be true,
never up for something new,
making me feel bad for the things I do,
making me wonder if I knew who
he was, really;
a blue, lying-to-you,
pretending-he-knew,
half-there boy all the way through;
a ghost in the last couple months
and I never even knew,
I guess I should have seen through
his deep, big blue.

dew, dew, dew

rain dripping on my skin,
my body is a sidewalk

I smell of water and renewal;
the heat in my thoughts creates fog that blurs my vision

until everything is a cloud—
push me around in it like it's a wagon

I want to water the flowers with my tears and
cry sunshine onto the grass that loves me…

tell me I'm worth it as I lie
between the trees

I am your sister, I am your mother,
you are my friend

picking fruit off of my arms
I have nothing it's all for you

I give and give and I give
and you wonder, we wonder

why I'm not beautiful
I am in, I am out

the dirt under my fingernails has rooted roses
and every now and then I can feel the trickle of the
watering can

spring cleaning

do you think
you could leave the door cracked
on your way out of my head?
I'll be in my room,
making my bed—
tidying the sheets,
fixing the mess we made
and trying to erase the muddy footprints
you tracked all around my brain.

I'll be opening the windows again,
to let out the smell of your skin
and let the light in;
playing the music you said was too loud
in hopes of drowning out the sound
of my heart
beating louder
and faster
as she realizes you're not coming back

trying

fold me in like a butterfly,
make my wings cover my eyes,
make me small again
and tuck me away inside your heart

I want to hear it beat like a drum,
pulse with it as I hear its echo,
look through the chambers like open windows
and feel what it's like to have purpose

then unhinge the lock from your chest and set me free
I'll fly up to your mind, to the sky
and try to carry with me the way that I felt when I was useful,
when I was loved,
just for the blink of an eye

rose is the saddest color

the sky is crying with me tonight,
but my tears have no purpose

there are no daisies to drink my water
like the ones dying outside my window

so I sit cross-legged in front of my mirror and stare
as I paint my cheeks with little roses that get stuck in my hair

and washed away by my showers
until all that is left is watercolor pink on pale skin,

my true color, the impostor falling down my face and dying
as it smacks the pavement of my legs

eyelashes

these broken windshield wipers
trying so hard yet failing
to keep everything clear

things I already knew about myself,
but somehow hearing them aloud
is worse than my constant storm of hypotheticals

hideous emotion, repulsive attraction
making my logical world foggy
so that the car of my mind swerves on its tracks

lost

I am a staircase that never ends,
turning, twisting, turning
until I am so dizzy that I must stop to rest.

I sit and cross my feet,
think about where I am,
and get up again.

up, up, up
it never ends.

steal me out of the deep, and
until then,
I'll just pretend to know where I am

or where I am going
or that I can keep on standing
without a single person to take my hand

either oil

rainbow in the oil on the street
mix it up, but keep it neat;
step out strong, but look both ways,
make sure when you fall, it's onto your knees;
speak up, speak up, but not too loud;
don't lose yourself in the crowded haze,
but don't feel the need to stand out

be authentic, be real,
but try not to give too much away

how is it a surprise
I can never stop thinking enough
to say

the same things you've always said

I wish you would stop telling me to shut my mouth
Stop telling me that my thoughts are just dust bunnies,
loose change, crumpled paper
found in the pockets of souls everywhere
only to be thrown away once they are remembered

Stop telling me that I'm not special,
that everyone likes to fall asleep to thunderstorms
and searches for flowers to stick their heads into

I wish that I could stop listening to you
because you are what is keeping me up at night
because you are a voice that never stops speaking
a voice I cannot tune out because maybe it is more appealing
to believe you are incapable
than to face your fears.

I wish that I could say your voice is not my own,
that I do not recognize your face,
that I could not pick out your tone in a sea of noise and
screams.

But I am you, and you are me.
I didn't fight you; I furnished you,
gave you a place to sleep inside my head
and blessed you with the roof of my skull.

We are one,
and each time my heart beats, you get bigger
as I shrink.

I feel you, always,
each time I breathe or try to think.
You suffocate my words and push them back down my throat
so that if I try again, I'll choke.

Maybe my words are meant to brew inside,
to ferment,
or maybe that's just you
again,
telling me the same things you've always said.

slow burn

jaw sewn tight together
by my anxious mind's needle
tongue of fire held inside, burning
my little mouth

I am a slowly spinning record,
afraid of playing music that is too loud

separation

stained glass eyes peering at me as I try to think
all of my decisions are exposed under the divine microscope
pick apart my thoughts, dissect me
and tell me what I'm worth;
can you see the morals in the broken puzzle pieces?
change the lens, put me into focus
leave me alone for a few days to grow
and when you come back, you'll know
the workings of this little soul

double vision

the day dragged me behind like her reluctant child,
the sun pulled me up like her puppet
and I saw the hours laid out before me
but still took twice as long to catch up to them and rest.
falling behind, can't figure out why,
today my sun set at half past nine

for M.

I know it breaks you
to see me broken

I'm sorry I couldn't do it on my own,
that I had to ask you to help me fill in the cracks

I promise I tried so hard to do it myself

but every time I bent down with the glue
another piece of me fell back down too

cracked glass,
trying to fill myself up with water
as I watched it flood my feet.

sinking

Sometimes I feel at peace with my place in the world. I can sit quietly in a room and not be noticed, I can relax in the notion of not being remembered as calmly as one sinks into a bubble bath. But some days I feel like a jaw clenching its teeth, like I've been clenching mine for days and just recognized its pressure all at once, on edge and energized with the frustration that comes from being invisible. I feel like a shard of glass, absorbing everyone else's light as they collectively stare right through me. Taking up all other colors, yet forever in the background. I wonder sometimes if there is something wrong with me that I feel so separated from everyone else, like a child peering into an exhibit at the zoo. Fascinated, intrigued, but destined to be an outsider—never on the inside, no matter how curious. My voice never seems to be loud enough, even when I scream, as if I am stuck in a deep valley while everyone else stands unaware at the top. I feel myself breathe, I hear myself think, think, think why am I not seen.

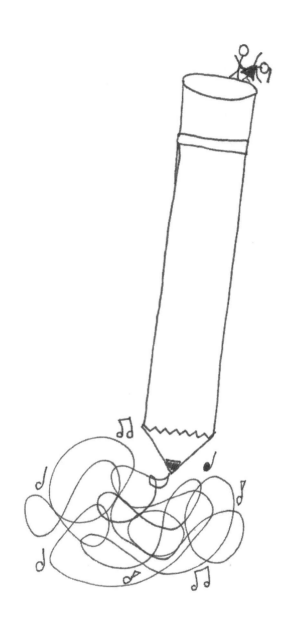

lead people dancing on my pencil eraser

there are lead people dancing on my pencil eraser,
leaving the dust of their graphite problems
as they twirl near the edge so close to breaking

bear down too hard and I'll snap you in half,
can't get a grip and my fingers will slip—
the stroke of my pencil does not match the beat of your waltz

scribble, scribble
jumbled words and music notes
until I fall asleep and you fall to the floor,
hitting my hanging shoelace
before you hit the white tile and
break

vertigo

scream!
as I sit here, straight-faced
as always,
shoelace dangling to the floor;
flick my foot side to side
because I don't feel anything anymore

scream!
in one ear, out the other;
I am the unforgiving
mother
of purpose and intent,
struggling
to make a dent in the
heaps of loving myself
and laundry and lethargy.
floating in a meadow of lavender,
sitting with the earth
because she isn't capable of indifference
toward me.

somebody scream at me,
wake me up;
it's more than enough,
I'll tell myself to wake up.

if

I see you and I see
all of the things I am not

so much confidence in such a small frame;
so much life in your name

I see how people look at you
and it sticks in my head

because I recognize it as an expression
that has never been how people look at me

you are happiness and air,
thought and beauty

I look at you and see all the things I cannot be;
you are me if I had decided to be free

beautiful lies

I listened to beautiful words
pour out of your lips

it's a shame they weren't true
but somehow, I couldn't hear anything else
and I didn't want to

hopes and fears

I kneel down beneath the stained glass
and close my eyes,
feel each ray pierce me as a different color of light

I pray that you make me a prism,
let me make something beautiful
from all the jumbled pieces of my life

crying
hoping
that each tear that hits the floor will make me feel clean and
loved

I came here
looking for something in the pews and hymnals,
maybe looking for myself

because I have finally admitted that I am a fraud.

I fake smiles when appropriate,
I am polite,
I speak only when I am spoken to

and when I am alone,
and have a few seconds to spare to breathe or think—
usually it's one or the other—

I hurt
for the girl who thought she would be something,
at the very least, herself.

but instead I hide in the backs of classrooms,
I drift to the walls of every room I enter,
so afraid to be in the unforgiving center

where I fear I will wobble and fall
and so I am a girl who still holds on to the edges of skating
rinks,
a girl who never lets anyone know what she thinks

eighteen years of containment,
holding my breath constantly,
caging all the butterflies that everyone else sets free.

of all the things in this world I could be scared of,
I never imagined the thing I would fear most is
being me.

CHRYSALIS

october

I want to curl up and run away,
go to sleep and let my body sway,
spend a year in dry dock and set out to sea.

I want to scream and I want to cry,
tear something apart and lie by your side,
change myself like a leaf on a tree.

I want to stand tall again and fall back down,
all I want is to feel at home in myself again, in my town.

a voice that I think
used to be a song)

wishful thinking

how can I be so fickle?
less than a month ago I loved you
and I think I still do,
just not in the way I used to.
I think I have fallen into a cycle,
taking advantage of how easy you make everything for me;
how easy you are to love,
just as easy to forget.
you put so much energy into loving me,
into being my light,
that I think I have begun to assume.
to assume that you love me
to assume that you think about me
to assume that these things will be true
even if I take a moment to myself
and seem to forget about you.
I fought for this, I cried over you,
and now, I accept you.
you, a voice in my head
that I have begun to tune out—
a voice that I think used to be a song

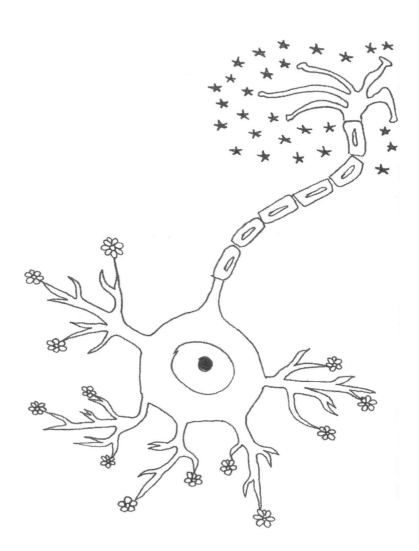

neurochemistry

you plant roses in my skull;
shooting up from my brain,
beautiful cerebellum,
stem entwined with stem.

the buds smell so sweet
that I ignore the bruises to my heart;
my synapses fire flowers
to each neuron and to the stars.

you grow on me like vines;
twisting and crawling and spreading
over my body until I don't remember
what's beneath the leaves or outside your touch.

stop sheltering me;
I cannot bear the ever-present ivy.
the roses in my head have turned yellow
like the sun my skin longs to drink in.

heliocentric

sometimes I look at you and think,
you're all I'll ever want,
but then I close my eyes and remember,
you're all I've ever had

not that I would change
a thing about us
but I wonder
if I would feel the same if you weren't the only sun in my life

what was the question?

do you ever feel like you've shared too much of yourself,
like you've given your whole heart when they asked only for
your hand?
I love without trying; it's involuntary

and it's like I have finally emerged
from this whirlwind of dust
and flower petals and feelings
that had lifted me up in a cloud of seeming happiness

so now I am falling
because I couldn't look down, couldn't see through
and when I hit the ground, I knew.
it is the same every time: I see them holding my heart in their
hands
and I feel like I have betrayed myself

subconsciously

It doesn't feel at all like destruction
You don't hear the broken bell even if it's ringing
In fact, it feels more like construction;
I can tell myself that I am building, singing

And with each stroke I am free,
Finally able to step off that cliff and over the edge,
Away from that mountain of thoughts that is too high up for
me to breathe,
And I can fall deeply, unconscious, into the nettles of my
mind's hedge.

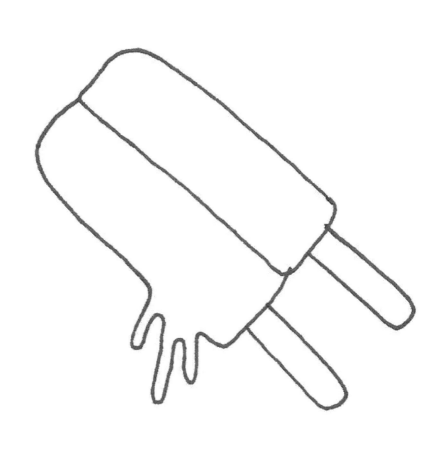

july

Stuck in the same rut
of wondering who cares and who
does not

Smothered by the stifling heat
that I breathe in
Every day feels like a Tuesday

Melted popsicle on the sidewalk
staining it red and then
erasing itself just as quickly

I am one with the sun;
I give light all day
but no one really looks at me

July, July
repeating itself
until I fold in on myself

I thought I had pulled myself
together

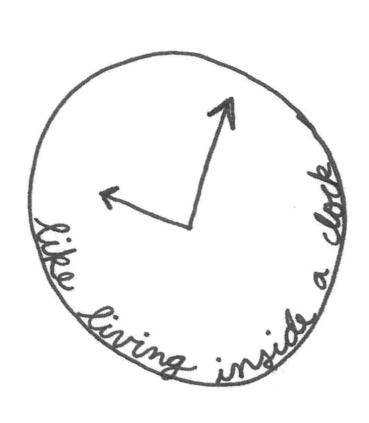

ringing

tonight, I can't sleep
so I'll focus on how slowly I can write
to see if it's better than counting sheep
I'm so used to having dark thoughts fill my head
that I've started to miss them
because lately in my mind, it's been low tide,
without moonlight, without sunlight—
just a bitter, tasteless in-between
that makes my tongue feel papery and dry;
it makes me think that the floods are better than the droughts

at least there was no sense of waiting before,
like living inside a clock

lie down with me by the ocean,
maybe if I get close enough I'll hear her voice again in the
shells
maybe I'll be able to stop, just for a minute,
talking only to myself

trapped

unbalanced, topsy-turvy world
I see through blue-tinted glasses,
will I always feel this way?
just about to cry, I am so stuck inside
myself, inside this head, inside this mind.
I wish that I could take my own hand
and tell myself it will all be okay,
that someone would reach down to pull me out
of this deep, deep well that is myself.

ode to nostalgia

I wonder

if I will always think of you
when Radiohead comes on shuffle,

why I feel like I am driving in your car again
every time I wear my old perfume,

when the last survivors of that October's butterflies
will finally fly away;

how long does the heart remember?

axis

some days I feel like I am flying, floating,
simple things like ladybugs and lakes make me elated
and hearing rugged hands on piano keys is enough
to make me cry with a wave of nostalgia
for a beautiful past I have not lived

and then I hear a snap, a crack, and I am flying, falling,
a thousand little ladybugs are crawling up my back
and I am drowning in every lake
and hearing dainty hands on piano keys is enough
to make me cry with the realization
that I have been living in black and white

what is a mind but a single ship on a fickle sea?
heaven and hell have joint custody of me

anxious

calling across that empty cave,
thinking you are alone,
but I sit inside,
covering my ears,
trying to shelter myself

from the noise,
from the shouts—
the noise that I think
is simply
a manifestation of my own doubts

I can hear you screaming at her,
your voice sounds like plates shattering.
why do you always stay in the loudest room of the house?
you ruin it, and it is always me left to clean up,
crying at the sink and scrubbing my mind with dish soap.

a part of me is afraid that you live here now,
that I can't tell you to move out.
closing my eyes never seems to help,
and it would take more than a thousand screams
to ever drown you out.

tick

I am starting to feel like a broken clock, out of place
Some days I remember the old rhythm, a feel and taste
of all the little things I used to be,
the little things that used to add up to me.

Time passes more slowly than it used to.
I've spent more nights just blinking to stay awake
and I've realized I don't feel the same
about things I thought would never change.

shell

feeling like a shell buried beneath the sand
as countless waves lap over me,
beating me, suppressing me,
suffocating me so rhythmically

maybe if I think about the sun,
I will feel it on my skin;
maybe if I don't think of the water,
drowning will become cleansing

maybe when I stop thinking,
I am

background music

blending in can be everything
a nice cream-colored wall like me lets the red couch
you just bought for the living room
really pop

the extras in the film you just watched,
people like that are paid to blend in.
maybe I should be too—
I do feel like it's my job sometimes

let them learn from me,
shadow the professional shadow,
follow me following the world,
become one with the no one

blending in can be everything
but what about when you have taken in too much,
without anyone, anywhere, to put it down?
who will wring you out?

then blending in becomes caving in very quickly
and the roof falls in on the bright red couch,
the camera inevitably approaches the star,
the sun sets and takes the shadows with her

maybe there is something more to life than blending in
I pray every day that I find it

ARE THE
FLOWERS
NO ONE
PICKS STILL
pretty?

quiet

I am a flower
dripping with sweet nectar
None of the bees notice
my soft petals peeking out from the blanket of grass
Is it my fault that my perfume is not as strong,
that my petals fold inward to hide from
the unforgiving sun?

The rays still touch me with their glowing fingers
through the scattered patches in the leaves
But I fear I will stay here in the shadows forever
while the world buzzes around me
Are the flowers no one picks still pretty?

physics

I need you out of my head!
I have to focus on other things,
and it's quite selfish of you to think
that you can waltz back in, playing
your music so loudly after all these months.

What is even more frustrating
is that I can't seem to tune it out,
and part of me still wants to dance with you.
I see you from across the room and I feel
so stupid, so stupid for feeling
what I feel, which is not something I can name.

So I must fold you up like a post-it note
and bury you in a drawer to collect dust
among my graveyard of worries;
I don't know why I am letting you rule my entire mindset,
like I am just a planet in inevitable orbit.

I guess that's what it all comes down to— physics, science,
the force that I feel but can't explain
because it is above my own understanding.
I thought time would help,
but gravity doesn't just disappear.

Maybe everything is acting on some level of inertia
that began when I hurled you away from me so suddenly;
I peered over the edge to see where you landed
and have been tumbling down that same hill toward you
ever since— I guess in that way, love is logic,
feelings are never really finite, missing you is just math.

Familiarity plus old emotions minus closure
equals this big, crazy number,
irrational and maybe imaginary,
a swarm of resurrected butterflies
in the pit of my stomach, a dancing heart, and a mouth
that wants so badly to scream and let it all flood out
until the weight of your name on the scale falls back to zero.

hurt

you do not hear me when I talk
you knock me back with incessant waves
that come back each time I get to my feet
I can't stand long enough to get out a sentence

you've taken over my mind
and reduced me to a shadow,
sitting in the corner of my own brain
trying to figure out if you've always been here

changing

I am supposed to be the bee
like I've always been

buzzing endlessly,
not stopping until there is honey

but lately there seem to be no flowers
left for me, like there is no color outside of me,

and I sit on the edge of my mind's hive,
thinking.

sandstorms

sometimes I let what I'm feeling
cloud everything else
like a sandstorm

until I am spinning furious clouds
with anxiety, fear,
insecurity, doubt.

they lift me up as they pull me down
and hurl me into corners of my mind
that make me feel scared and alone.

I start speaking languages
I didn't know that I knew,

then I am running so fast and so far from
myself that I trip and fall every time
and fall asleep from the exhaustion.

I wake up
and everything is clear again.

I realize that the sky was clear before, too—
it is always me who stirs up these winds,
creating storms for myself
and placing myself as the tallest tree in this vast field;
surrounding myself with everyone else;
letting all of this horrible heat and relentless wind rage.

then I watch myself try to rebuild, just to see if I still know how.

undeveloped

looking at you feels like seeing a photograph in off lighting;
same blue shirt you always wore on Saturdays
but different from how I remembered it,
same bit of hair sticking up from your head, just above your eye
but now it seems out of place,
same face from before, but you aren't you anymore

maybe we are still soaking in a solution somewhere,
and how things used to be will be preserved at least as long as it
takes for us to dissolve
but the person you are now doesn't remember me;
the negatives never developed into color,
so we will always be just one moment that could never fully
bloom into another

she

she sits at the bottom of the ocean,
a sculpture of God, calcified from the tears she cried,
brought out of the water, excavated
by a thousand tiny hands
that crawl over her in places she is used to being vacant
hands that try to find meaning in the curves and lines

she cannot speak, tell them their flaws in searching for hers
her lips have hardened from disuse
and she is exposed, naked
just as trapped on land as under the weight of the ocean,
now oxidizing in the open air

she could have stayed hidden,
an underwater garden kept secret from those who love her,
but I can't stand the pressure building in my ears
after being so completely submerged for all these years

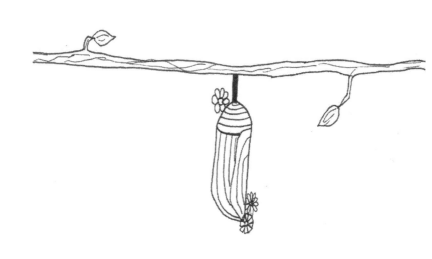

cocoon

fresh out of the womb, screaming, pouting,
I am still just a caterpillar, born late but too soon.
wrap me up in a blanket that makes me feel warm again,
makes me feel at home again, my new cocoon.

four years old, bright eyes,
I cry every day my mother leaves me;
I am still in my shell, haven't learned yet how to yell.
take me home in my blanket that makes me feel like myself,
like I don't need to talk so much like everyone else.

time moves slowly but so fast,
painting the sidewalk and a couple of arm casts,
realizing I no longer like math,
birthdays and sleepovers and all these days that passed—

then nothing changes except everything,
I am surrounded by beautiful wings,
everyone fluttering, hovering, soaring
above me in a rush of color as I am stuck inside
my safety blanket, my shell, my head,
this same blank, white, cracked cocoon.

I DAYDREAM   I IMAGINE

I AM STAGNANT

guilt

I carry it with me on my shoulder,
a rock that doesn't slip off when I laugh,
pushing me down when all I want is to float
or at least come up for air

but I asked for this boulder,
I am not the constellation everyone thinks I am,
connected in all the right places
so I make sense

my stars are disconnected in some places,
dim where others shine,
and I think you focus on the little glimpses of light
rather than the dark blanket that is their background

I daydream, and I imagine, and I am stagnant

I never make progress,
I want to feel clean again,
but I am so confused.
who gave me my set of values?

blooming

I thought that I could be a flower. That if only I placed myself
in the right conditions, the right environment, I would bloom
inevitably, with the sureness and force of a meteor heading
for Earth. I imagined myself as the botanist, planting myself,
tweaking little dials of sunlight and spotlight, or water and
nourishment. I thought that I could understand it, like I always
do; I thought that I could make recreating myself into a
science, that I could plot my own growth on a plane. But
everything is not as easy as experiments— I am still myself,
without a single sprout or leaf. Maybe I am not meant to
bloom. Or maybe the root of it all is comparison— it's difficult
not to feel you are a weed in a garden of roses. It's not my fault
I want to shrink, but sometimes I get the sense that the others
feel I am ivy, crawling over and around them so they have no
room to breathe. I thought that I could change myself, but
perhaps it's just that the seed of a sunflower can never grow
into a dainty daisy. I can still be a flower, but only if I give
myself time to grow.

wednesday

chipped nail polish,
cracked knuckles,
mind forgetting to sleep

thinking about old songs I used to like,
the hearts that I used to hold,
and the things I thought defined me

maybe what's broken is meant to drift out at sea
and we are more like our past than we ever intended to be

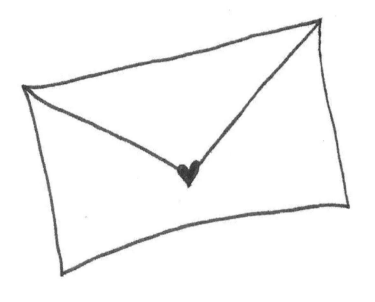

hallmark

he never stops begging me to let him tell me how he feels,
pleading that he didn't get to say what he should have;
but each time he hits play and lets this monologue run on loop,
he wastes an opportunity
as I carve another tally mark into the wall

I am walking toward a sun that blinds him
as he tries to chase me,
he will never know what it feels like to pour out his heart
because all he ever does is send me blank greeting cards,
and I am expected to find meaning in the emptiness

surreal

a painted face and a blue heart
glowing from the rain within,
floating on clouds that could fall through in an hour

when I hit the earth
and sink into it,
I have to crawl my way out,
heels sticking in the soil on the way to the sun

branching trees, slanted streets,
I cannot find my way back to the heart;
gusts of wind carry all these selfish sins,
music does sound sweet when upside down

set right again,
clouds let the light back in,
only a few more steps
on the staircase to the stars

balloons

cold feet, warm hands
everything is the opposite of what it should be
I look at you and somehow everything is different
but still the same

my stomach sinks with the weight of you
but I am lifted up by balloons filled with the same air
from thirteen months ago

you would think they would have deflated by now
(I know I have)
but I feel so heavily light, so happily sad,
so hopeful and confused

shock me with this air
or pop this balloon I have been holding
in my hands for too long
this state of floating in between is making me run out of breath

rebuilding

sometimes I get the idea that in my head I am
constantly, subconsciously, trying
to tape over the old recordings of you

I see something that reminds me of you, I think,
but it's faint— an old song that I can remember
only a few notes of, not the tune

maybe my mind is protecting me, rebuilding
on top of what is lost, creating new memories
that cover up thoughts of you

like a canopy over a rainforest floor—
a layer of thick green leaves that intertwine like fingers
but can't ever stop all of the light from shining through to the
foundation below.

inside out

there are two of me
inside my head right now

the logical me, the one I've always known
to be myself,

and this impostor, always whispering to me,
but she has started to look and sound like me

right now, I can still tell them apart,
but they are always fighting for my attention

one telling me I am not good enough, listing a thousand things
for me to worry about, to cry over

the other held underwater until the last second
until she can finally rise to the surface and scream

foggy

he doesn't deserve to know!
but he is all I have.
no, I don't owe him anything,
but I still want to open myself up.

this is my problem:
I always give, give, give,
throwing myself into others' arms
without taking the luxury of a second thought.

I know that this is because I am hurting,
because I have been feeling this emptiness inside me
for so long that I am searching for anyone to grab onto,
like I have ten seconds left on an imaginary clock.

desperation is no excuse to overshare,
I cannot let myself slip into old habits
just because I need someone to hold me and listen;
I am worth more than I feel right now,
I am not an emotional sell-out.

happy machine

Some days I feel the need to zoom in
and zoom out from myself;
gain a new perspective, find a new angle, another direction,
simply because what stands is not working.

I want to know what causes this intense happiness,
to see what fireworks, dances, sunrises
are taking place behind my eyes

and if they are strong enough to sustain themselves
or if I will soon return to the familiar feeling of falling down—
trying to swim in an empty pool,
laughing but not hearing myself,
not being able to cry.

What is it that makes this mind tick?
Take me inside to look at the gears that I know can run so
smoothly
but like to rust from time to time.

blurry winter

what is this pearl in my throat,
this out-of-place feeling
that I seem to put on each morning like a coat

I am just a girl,
trying to discover herself
and feel grounded in a life like a tilt-a-whirl

call my name, and I'll turn around,
closing my eyes, praying that when I open them
someone will see me, save me, finally found.

on my time

trying to trap this feeling in a glass
like a lightning bug captured in the lazy drone
of a summer evening,
or a laugh caught on camera

I spend my mornings swimming up to the surface
of my night's dreams,
my days pressing flowers picked in the early morning light,
my nights writing about how I spent my days

sometimes it makes me wonder
what it is that makes the past seem so beautiful
but a wonderful detachment from the present
and a fear of the future

shotgun state of mind

I am filling to the brim
with indecisiveness;
half of me hoping that I'll overflow
and tip over
if falling is the only way to choose a side

like picking the most beautiful planet,
I spin around and around,
create a blur of the stars
and see different expressions of the same wonderful feeling;
I can't decide

who put me in charge of my own universe?
not with this ready storm of a mind—
I watch flowers die because I wait too long to pluck them.
I never learn that I am driving, not just along for the ride.

dizzy

At night I awake
Time to paint the walls
Go to sleep, go to sleep—
try to tear down the clock.
I see other people
already washing their brushes;
The day is done,
colors flush down sinks in pink rushes

But here I am all alone
A blank heart, a blank canvas,
no one around to give me a map or spare compass
Why am I always late, late, late?
I hear laughter in the next room,
but once I get there,
they've closed the gate.

Back to my room, back to my mind
with everything else that's been left behind—

Swirling in my own lazy galaxy
of fear, doubt, and anxiety;
I try to look at the stars, but they blind me.

I fear the world is moving too fast for me
and that everything happens at the exact moment I decide to
rest my eyes...
Awake, awake,
the world doesn't wait.

WINGS

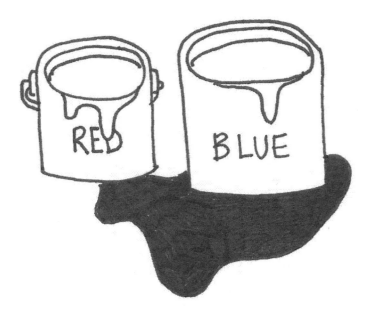

purple is not a primary color

My feelings are not meant to be categorized,
filed under happy,
sad,
angry,
upset disappointed jealous
or any other word you can think of
to try to define what's inside of me

It's a crime telling me
I can't color outside the lines
because all that I'm feeling
is not meant to be separated with brick walls in my brain;
Everything runs together

like paint cans spilling
onto the garage floor, ruining the newspaper
you laid down so it wouldn't get messy

Emotions aren't like that;
your newspaper will get ruined,
and your mind will get messy
with all the paint you tried so hard not to spill

But then you see all the new colors it made,
so it's okay that you cried for an hour
before you realized
you needed both the red and the blue
to create the purple that's touching your toes

great wall of silence

I have always built up a wall of flowers around myself
Thick enough to hide behind, but still peek through,
Letting others come by when they need a rose or two

Learning to love the rain and what it gives me,
Loving to learn what I can give others from between the blades
of grass

plant me in your soul

plant me in your soul
I may not bloom right away,
but I will nourish you;
I will give you life, I will give you love

all I ask
is you give me light
and a place to stay,
I will reciprocate

take me in
and I will take root in your heart
if you wait long enough for my petals
to unfold

prayer for rain

Coming out on my own
I feel a new need for you,
like you have loosely knotted my heart to a rope
and have been pulling it toward you
so that my head is turned to look to the clouds
and see you again

atlas

on days like this I stare up at the clouds
and watch them inch across the blue,
moving so slowly
because they are dragging my worries away with them too

beginnings

The stone tossed in the pond effects
a silent earthquake

The pool of clear water cannot quite hide
the tree's infinite snaking roots

The flowers shoot up to the sky,
their yellow petals misty in the morning rain

All the earth blooms around me,
yet still I think only of you

blue

you are my blue
peaceful as the sky
on a cloudless day
bright as the warm summer rain
calm as the sea
before a night storm
you are blue, blue
everything blue
car parked in front of my house
flowers in the front seat
rain jacket in the dining room
everything is always so beautifully blue with you
like the rain I always want to come
somehow even your brown eyes sing blue to me

porcelain and clay

Every other night I'm porcelain
but tonight I'm made of clay;
I don't know why my perfectly made-up face can't think
of what to say when you look at me that way

I look at you, your eyes dark like the dock,
lips pink like my cheeks
and I think of us in your parked gray car
and its fake leather seats

You make me let my guard down
and I always let you in—
again you make me clay,
melting my porcelain.

higher

in all things, look up—
to gain a new perspective,
to see the clouds, the stars,
to ask for help,
to know who you want to become

composting

in my mind there is clay
of words, of emotions
that I use to create from things that make me feel like nothing

it's stored on the shelves,
always ready for me to make awake
like a color-by-number

but with you it's one step deeper—
there is no clay that quite matches
the color I feel when I think about you

so I must start from scratch, sift through the subconscious soil
and gather what broken eggshells of feelings
remain near the decaying roots

you make me create new clay
you give my mind a challenge
because you are not easily described

you remind me of how insufficient language can be,
that the truest words are not found on the surface;
and for that, I am thankful

recognition

that day I broke
all the tears inside of me found their way out
and watered the dying roses on my skin

it seemed as if I cried for days
reversing the drought of acceptance
and allowing myself to grow again

the shift

rising in the morning,
I dream of other things.
I am suddenly repulsed
by the scent of your roses;
I prefer the grass and the trees.
you start lightning inside of me
just as often as you make me smile,
thunder as often as laughs.
you tell me to relax,
but I was not made to be
the thing of silence that you see.
you make me feel guilty
about things I should not be sorry for;
rising in the morning,
I do not think of you anymore.

thursday morning

this is beautiful rain
the kind I can hear, feel,
but not always see
the kind that hits my cheeks,
crying for me
the kind that takes my burdens away
as it evaporates

flowering fantasies

there is a small place inside my head
where my dreams are harbored.
the sky is soft, pink cotton
blended with smooth blue silk.
a small ship sails on serene seas,
carrying my thoughts to and from
the different ports of my mind.
the sails are thousands of
full, blooming flowers
that blush pink and slowly sink
to the gentle water as my eyelids
flutter shut. the winds blow lightly over the calm water,
taking my dreams where they wish to go.
the pale mountains sing soft sweet music
that drifts along the waves
and through my head like a breeze.
this beautiful blossom of a ship will always sail
through the waters of my mind,
its captain never sparing time to look at anything
she has left behind.

empty space

shut the front door quietly in the morning
on your way out of my head

every other time you slam it: I hear it in my heart,
and my brain wakes up to an empty bed

you must understand how it feels, all the brand-new starts,
recreating myself and trying to forget everything you ever said

this time, when you leave, maybe I will get a full night's sleep,
and I'll wake up to the sound of a bird singing instead

cherries

look up—
not at the sun,
but just before it

cherries,
red, ripe, rare

but you never noticed them

until you had nothing else to eat
and needed something sweet

look at the cherries,
just out of your reach

I am just out of your reach

floating

on top of my mountain,
I feel nothing and everything;
flowering lungs that breathe in peace
and exhale everything that's been building up inside of me;
golden sunlight striking the blue-green sea
that is my best friend's eyes,
rock that is solid and smooth
and holding me up above it all, despite it all;
surrounded by calmness and beauty and quiet,
a thousand reminders of how small my worries are
back on the ground

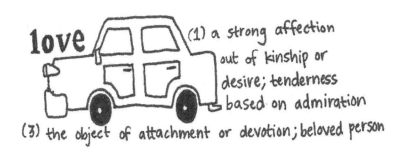

love (1) a strong affection out of kinship or desire; tenderness based on admiration (3) the object of attachment or devotion; beloved person

parts of speech

We lived in parts of speech, in adjectives thrown around
without meaning, racing cars that looked like terms of
endearment but were really just empty air. We jumped around
the thesaurus, floated on blank notes, walked along the
definition of a word in the dictionary so that our feet covered
the meaning. We sent letters in a language we didn't
understand even though we thought we did. Because of you,
I have realized that loving someone isn't just saying you do; it's
feeling, doing, touching, running, believing, too.

hands that sculpt

close my eyes and imagine I am creating myself
painting my lips with the dust of a rose
sculpting my fingers, molding my nose
whispering into my ears the same breath that I exhale

wondering what I would change if I could be both the artist
and the art, constantly creating

but this is what I am every day,
always on display,
with hands that sculpt and a mind of clay

let me be the artist I admire
creating for no purpose other than to make
let me form my thoughts the way I would paint a watercolor
bright, beautiful, not afraid to run together
let me create myself as I've always wished to be
fully living, fully breathing, me

summer sun

the warm sunlight flows lazily from the window and finds its way to me like a magnet— I can see it dance on the wooden floor, moving back and forth like humming flowers or a plucked string that creates a note of perfect pitch— this summer sun knows me, hears the silent sound of my tears escaping my eyes, and seeps in through every crack, every hole, every window, until I am bathing in it, this lovely new skin that is warm and happy, and I can see colors in the golden rays that call me daughter

places I've never been

I dream of faraway places,
where language is a spoken art
and people make beautiful little things
with hands that tell stories and eyes that make me believe them.

I hear my name as it is carried through the trees,
as it echoes in the cold winds—
a chorus of voices that sounds like culture
and beauty and excitement.

Their calls reach me from across the seas
and whisper in my ear whenever my mind is blank;
They color my thoughts and bring them to life
with the wonders of places that I've never been.

I cannot keep from singing

Let the ants crawl over my feet like they are mountains, let the
wind flow through my hair. The flowers on my skin long for
the sun's sweet nectar. I want to match pitch with the voices
of the mountains; my heart wishes to beat in sync with great
rolls of thunder as my God washes this sweet earth with endless
showers of redemptive rain.

cold hands, warm heart

last night, I dreamt of you—
we were in the car, it was snowing,
and each snowflake that stuck to the windshield
was prettier than you think I am

I don't know who you are,
what your name is;
I can't remember your face
but I can't wait to meet you

soft spot

a little bit of you sleeps inside my heart
and a little bit of me sleeps inside yours
you can still make me feel like I'm floating;
seeds sown a long time ago start to bloom again when I see you
you were my first, and you make me feel seen
there is nothing so beautiful and so strange as history

perspective

Today was the first time I heard a Smiths song
playing on the radio— on the way home
I drove past the dock,
and it was the first time the words "where I had my first kiss"
popped into my head
with the impartial tone of a tour guide.

There must be something to the fact
that now I remember to wear sunglasses when I drive,
that I can look at my old emotions
as things of beauty
without being consumed by them, by my old self.

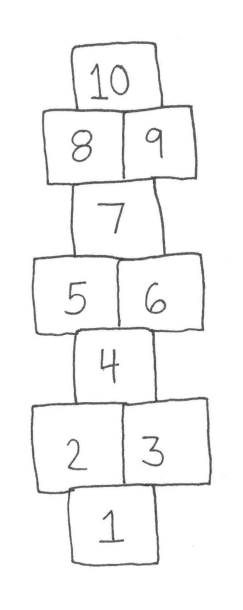

walking home

I love the sound of laughter,
of feet pounding sidewalks
as we run from all our overwhelming worry
or race toward our biggest joys—

How wonderful it is to be so little,
yet to feel such great, crushing things.

some things stay the same

when I wanted to change the color of my hair
and snip everything I'd ever done off at the root,

when I cried for six days out of seven
and saw that as a failure too,

you showed me the watercolor skies
and did something I never could do

you let me see that some things stay the same
when the rest of the world is spinning,
and all I can say is thank you

lost/found

I want to be lost,
the sole flower in thickets of grass,
only to be stumbled upon by lovers in the golden afternoons;
the melody that floats through your head but cannot be named;
the book that sits dusty on the shelf, collecting light on its gilded
pages

I want to be found,
but only by the one
who notices me sitting among the trees
and does not see me as hiding;
the one who wonders how no one has seen me out in the open;
the one who can't help thinking
I am a figment of the imagination
brought on by the same summer sun that made me

I am lost
so that when I am found
it can only be you

sounds

like a breeze blowing through cornflowers,
like honey swirling into hot tea,
like hushed footsteps in the quiet morning,
like a reverence for words and what they can do;
sounds like a voice I'd love to keep listening to.

purple light

I am drunk on this buzzing energy,
the freedom I feel in anonymity

pull me closer to your heart,
the one who knows me, let's go back to our start

I hear all the sounds of being young tonight
and I am not scared because it's you by my side

although this is not forever, not something that you mean,
I am okay with this feeling of being wanted and being seen

joie de vivre

there is life all around me;
I breathe in grass and plant my feet in watered soil,
then I run with the sea salt breeze that chases me
like long-echoing laughter.

it has taken me a long while
to realize, but I have opened my eyes
and know now that my body is change, beauty, and growth—
seed, blossom, and sapling all at once.

I am new, I am my true self,
I am golden skin, bright eyes, lovely,
born again, butterfly, garden,
weeping at how connected everything is.

metamorphosis

he is sweet, sugar
sitting on the porch
telling me about what makes me myself,
and the hesitation,
it melts in the silence
like the sugar in the water
that I leave out for the butterflies
who inhabit my dreams' backyard

so this time I will let them sip on it
instead of telling them they don't deserve it

let them become drunk on your words,
fluttering behind my eyes—
the steady beating of their wings makes them feel beautiful,
and no longer deprived

ACCEPT ALL THE
LITTLE THINGS

YOU'RE MADE OF
& grow

the best that I can

this is not me, I think
as I cry uncontrollably
from all the doubt and all the worry
I have offered a home inside of me

but I have given it time,
I have given it my prayers and my hope,
and realized that sometimes it is better
to simply accept all the little things you're made of
and grow